A History of Dr. Frederick LaMotte Santee and the Coven of the Catta

Written and Compiled by
Gary Lee Hoke
ZAXON Publishing

ISBN # 978-0-557-85997-9

Quotes – Some are from the Harvard Yearbook 25th anniversary of the class of 1924. The quoted notes from the master's thesis are from a document I found in the library, author unnamed.

Photo credits – Many are by the author. Some were given to me by Lady Phoebe. Others are listed with their credits, or with no credits where I have not been able to trace the photographer.

Acknowledgements - I would first like to thank Tabatha Ferrell for lighting a fire under my butt to get me to finally write this book after it sat as rough notes for years. Thanks to Adonis Merlin for help with proofreading and photo editing. And thanks to Tony Oliveri for showing me how to edit this in Word for the publisher and for his encouragement.

This author takes full responsibility for any mistakes made in the writing of this book.

Table of Contents

Introduction

On this All Hallows Samhain 31 October 2010, now almost 30 years after the death of Dr. Frederick LaMotte Santee and the beginning of my involvement in the Coven of the Catta of Wapwallopen Pennsylvania and beyond, I am writing what I know of this history.

Contact with the Coven of the Catta

We arrived at the book house of the late Dr. Santee's in 1981. My witch girlfriend and I had seen an ad in Circle Network News about a coven located in Wapwallopen, about 100 miles northeast of where we resided outside of Harrisburg Pennsylvania. We arrived and were led into his 50,000 volume book house where we were greeted by three elder ladies, Janee the High Priestess, Jeannie and Judy sitting in rocking chairs around a roaring fireplace flanked by large iron cauldrons. It couldn't be more archetypal "witchy".

They denied having placed that ad and were amazed at our arrival.

Santee Bookhouse Fireplace © GLH

We arrived there one year after Dr. Santee's death and everything was in disarray. The temple was full of items salvaged from Santee's house and the book house had suffered a fire that year which left a hole in the roof. We asked for teaching and initiation and Janee aka Edna Jane Kishbaugh-Williams aka Lady Phoebe Athene Nimue (acronym Lady PAN) accepted us. Their mood was somber as they had lost the center of their coven, Dr Frederick LaMotte Santee aka Lord Merlin, their High Priest. I will speak much more on him later.

Biography of Lady Phoebe

Here is a short biographical note on Lady Phoebe. She was an amazing lady. Phoebe or Janee was the High Priestess of the remaining coven members and is the witch who taught and initiated me. She was born in Berwick Pennsylvania on 13 April 1921. She met Dr. Santee in 1956 and was his receptionist-secretary at the Santee Medical office and Santee Memorial Library in Wapwallopen, Pa. They both had married partners but they were each other's platonic soul mates. She had no children. She was afflicted with a degenerative arthritic disease which left her body twisted, one leg shorter than the other and her nose was replaced with an artificial one. Of course like all of Santee's girls she wore high heels even in her condition.

Lady Phoebe circa 1965
Courtesy Dave Hoag

I obtained a lot of old photos from 1965 of Santee's girls and they were all in high heels, skirts just above the knee, faux fur coats and cat's eye glasses. Phoebe was an artist from a young age and she actually met Lady Alsace or Jeannie at a painting class. She drew a lot of the illustrations and wrote poetry and invocations for the Coven. Here are some of her and Santee's works.

Lady Triumphant from the Cat's Tale

I AM HE

Like a god I can wipe away the clouds from the sky if you want it blue. I will pull down the stars to light your room at night if you want me to. Tomorrow I will level off the mountains and drain the seas to make room for the palaces I have planned for you. Like a wall I stand between you and anything that might threaten your joy and peace. The kings and captains of the earth will wait outside to adore you on your new throne. While I live your will is law. The magic power I draw from you makes me invincible. There is nothing I cannot learn or do, no problem I cannot solve if you let me do it in your name and for your sake. The world has no existence for me apart from you. It has no meaning but what you give it. You are the cause and the purpose of all my deeds. If you leave me, my world will fall apart. Unless some other SHE comes quickly to the rescue, I shall die. To renew my strength, I have only to look upon you or touch you, and I go forth conquering in your name. What is it in you that revives and inspires me? I call it beauty. But this is only you creating and expressing yourself. For you are SHE.

Frederick

"I am He" by Santee

I AM SHE

I walk with you in the twilight that falls like fairy dust around us. My silvery robe and midnight blue cape swings in the gentle wind of the Gods.
No matter my gait, no matter whether I be slim or obese or my beauty be the beauty of 18 or 80 for I always walk straight and tall, my slim legs twinkling under the cob-web silk of my robe. I am always willowy as the figure of She and my beauty is forever.
I willingly allow you to be my wall between danger and my-self. I willingly allow you to worship at my shrine. You have earned that privilege of adoring at my feet for I am She. You can do naught without me. The vieled Isis can be unvieled to you only if I am at your side.
But I need you in order to be She. Without you I will be nothing as you are without me. With your strength and my beauty we will face and conquer the twilight of our world without fear. For you are he.

Janee

"I am She" by Phoebe

Lady Phoebe Athene Nimue

Edna Jane Kishbaugh Williams © GLH

She wrote a column in the local newspaper called "The Witches Kettle". She also wrote and edited the Coven's publication entitled "The Cat's Tale". In 1967 she and Dr. Santee were initiated by Sybil Leek. Phoebe has said that she remembers previous lives, one of which was the wife of an Indian chief who lived along the Susquehanna river hundreds of years ago. She was a strong wiled Aires and we did not always agree on everything, but she was my mentor who taught me how to be a witch and a Priest. She passed away on 5 December 2005 at the age of 84 and is buried in the Pine Grove Cemetery in Berwick, Pa.

Edna Kishbaugh Williams

Former aide to doctor enjoyed drawing

Edna Kishbaugh Williams, 84, formerly of 531 E. Fourth St., Nescopeck, died 12:03 p.m. Monday, Dec. 5, 2005, in Berwick Retirement Village II.

Edna was born in Berwick, April 13, 1921, a daughter of the late Edgar and Mary Slusser Kishbaugh.

She attended the former Nescopeck High School.

She retired as a receptionist-secretary with the late Dr. Frederick L. Santee, Wapwallopen, after his death in 1980.

She enjoyed drawing.

She was preceded in death by her husband, Dale Williams, on Feb. 22, 1998, and by two brothers: Ethan and Ralph Kishbaugh.

She will be remembered by nieces and nephews and their families.

Private services will be held with the Rev. Rodney Miller, pastor of Wesley United Methodist Church, Nescopeck, officiating. She will be laid to rest next to her beloved husband in Pine Grove Cemetery, Walnut Street, Berwick.

Obituary of Edna Jane Kishbaugh Williams

Grave of

Edna Jane Kishbaugh Williams © GLH

History of the Coven of the Catta

The Coven of the Catta was formed around 1967 by Santee and Phoebe as I shall call them from here on. They both loved cats and supported the Humane Society and gave the coven the totem of the cat "Bastet" from Egypt. Santee had been familiar with many in the occult world including Sybil Leek. They met in NYC and she was invited to Wapwallopen.

When Sybil arrived at the covenstead, according to Phoebe, she and the doctor's secretary-librarians asked her to teach and initiate them into witchcraft to form a coven. Sybil's lineage was from the Coven of the Horsa from the New Forest area SE of London England. She also hung out with and learned a lot from the Gypsies and their magickal ways. Before that the lineage came from Coven of the Red Dragon in Gorge de Loup (Wolf Gorge) in SE France. Santee himself, as I shall expand on later, carried a handful of witchcraft and occult lineages from Europe. The combination became the Coven of the Catta. At first they had their temple in the cellar of Santee's house.

Santee House Cellar Temple 1970

Sometime in the 1970s Dr. Santee had a cinder block building built right next to his house and doctor's office. Over the years he amassed a library that contained 50,000 books on all manner of subjects, from the Greek and Latin classics he loved to history and religion, including a fairly large occult section. There was the main room with fireplace and his large desk, another room with a round table for classes, a strong vault for the really old tomes dating back to the 17th century, and in the back a room used for rituals. After the bookhouse was built, they moved their temple from the old to the new one in full ceremonial garb. From 1967 to 1980, the year of Santee's death, the coven flourished with mostly members from the local community. In fact the Coven and the Doctor are somewhat of an urban legend in the area now with rumors of Satanism and cat sacrifices! The fact is they were just practicing good ole white witchcraft from everything I can see. They also published a newsletter called "The Cat's Tale" in which various articles, spells and pictures were submitted by the main coven members. These articles were written with a typewriter back then and mimeographed for circulation. I wrote articles for this newsletter on my 1987 era Mac computer, which at the time was oh so high tech. This just reminds me how far we have come, from having to write letters on paper and mail them to people to nowadays where witches communicate through their email, blogs, social media sites and websites.

In 1979 someone broke into the bookhouse to steal some of the doctor's

16th century books and gold and silver bars, then set fire to the place to cover it up. The resident cat Bastet was killed in the fire but left this mark. The place never fully repaired and the doctor died the next year.

$500,000 fire loss

This interior photograph of a portion of "The Book House" of Dr. Frederick Santee, Wapwallopen physician, shows some of the thousands of volumes that were burned or ruined by fire Tuesday evening. Although insured for $300,000, the area doctor estimated the loss at in excess of $500,000. Many of the books, collected for more than 50 years, were rare Greek and Latin volumes. Some of the books dated back to the 17th century. A state police fire marshal indicated the blaze may have been caused by a defective electric plug on a coffee machine. An investigation into the fire is continuing. The 71-year-old physician said, "It's like seeing a lifetime fall in and crash around you," as he looked over the debris. (Staff Photo)

Wapwallopen fire destroys valuable book collection

A Tuesday evening fire at a building adjacent to the home of Dr. Frederick Santee, Wapwallopen, destroyed or seriously damaged thousands of volumes of rare and valuable books.

A three-section, concrete block structure constructed by the Wapwallopen physician was known as "The Book House." Reports indicated that fire of undetermined origin began in an annex near the rear of the main library building. The fire was centered near a furnace and refrigerator, it was said.

Flames were discovered at about 6 p.m. Tuesday and by the time firemen arrived at the scene the fire had eaten through the ceiling and portions of the roof.

It was indicated that approximately 500,000 volumes were stored in the Santee private library. Many were first edition publications while others were rare Greek and Latin writings.

The collection of books had been the work of the 71-year-old physician and was widely known and used as a research center for scholars throughout the eastern United States.

Dr. Santee is the third generation of his family to practice medicine in the community of Wapwallopen.

A state police fire marshal has been called in to assist in the probe of the blaze.

No damage estimate was available at press time Wednesday.

7-5-9

Local article about the bookhouse fire

Outline of Bastet Cat © GLH

And that brings us up to 1981 when my Priestess Lady Iska Nuit Aradia and I arrived. Over the next few months we drove almost a hundred miles north, cleaned out the temple, re-painted the three circles as prescribed, and rituals began again with some people from that area and mostly witches who came up from the Harrisburg area 8 times a year for Sabats. I drove up even more often to hand copy my own three "Books of Shadows" from Lady Phoebe's two books, which is over 300 pages of material. Unfortunately when she passed all her possessions, including these books, were just thrown into the dumpster. Most of the material is from the books on witchcraft available in the 1970s, and the rituals mostly from Lady Sheba's Books of Shadows. What Phoebe taught was what is called today "Old Guard Wicca". We were taught to do the rituals as they were written in the books with no additions or subtractions. I suppose it is similar to a Catholic doing the Mass over and over. It may sound boring but there is a certain comfort in this type of ritual. The rituals for the Sabats were almost exactly alike except for short lines and ritual actions that were specific to the season. When it was time for our third degree initiation in which we were supposed to write our own ritual, Phoebe was not pleased with what we put together because it was too far off the original rituals. Away from the Sabats we would often drive up and take Phoebe out into the woods at special places she loved. We would go up on Council Cup the nearby mountain and in the picture above she taught us how to call the winds by whistling for them. She felt close to her AmerIndian past life and would tell us stories about it. At one place where her father had helped build an old stone bridge, out in the woods, she showed us the white spirit snake named "Sheesha" that Sybil had passed on to her, and that spirit was passed on and integrated into my magicke. One thing about the COC system is that there is a lot of physical work between Probationership and the First degree and it does take a year and a day. In fact, that time period is between all the degrees. There are instruments to be made and found and consecrated. You can't just buy everything on the internet like nowadays. We got blisters and bleeding fingers cutting our wands and besoms. For 9 years (1981-1990) we led a coven of many members who came and went. We and a handful of other witches were initiated into our higher degrees over time. I will detail these initiations at the end of this article.

HPT Shawnus Merlin Belarion

Covenstead Temple 1980s

My Priestess and I eventually parted ways. Due to witch politics I eventually withdrew from being High Priest of the Coven and let things wane down, as they did. I had my fallings out with Lady Phoebe at times, but eventually was also reconciled with her a few years before her death. Phoebe lost possession of the doctor's house and bookhouse and the latter fell into a more dilapidated state. I started doing the rituals again in her presence with Lady Alsace Isa Brie, an early elder member of the coven, as my Priestess. She is an Australian, a gifted psychic and wonderful gardener. We do these rituals mostly outside a couple times a year on her hilltop property outside Berwick, Pa. Sadly Lady Phoebe passed in 2005 and now the celebrants who come are mostly witches from other lineages and pagan friends.

High Priestess Lady Alsace Isa Brie

I also started having Lady Alsace down to my place north of Harrisburg to celebrate Sabats, usually at All Hallows. I have a temple set up on the first floor and in the cellar for larger groups. Witches from other lineages are freely invited and do come to these rituals.

HPT Shawnus Merlin Belarion 2003

Shawnus Cellar Temple 2010

A Biography of
Dr. Frederick LaMotte Santee

At his point I will write all I know about Dr. Santee, which is from Phoebe's stories, some articles I found in the Santee Memorial Library and from the Harvard Yearbooks. I never met him, having arrived one year after his passing, but he was an amazing man, doctor, scholar and occultist.

He was born 17 September 1906 in Wapwallopen, Pa. He was born in a lineage of four generations of doctor's who practiced medicine. His grandfather was a Civil War surgeon who helped runaway slaves. His father was Charles LaMotte Santee who held MD degrees from LaFayette and Jefferson colleges in 1901 and he passed away in 1963. His mother was Verna Caroline Lloyd Santee.

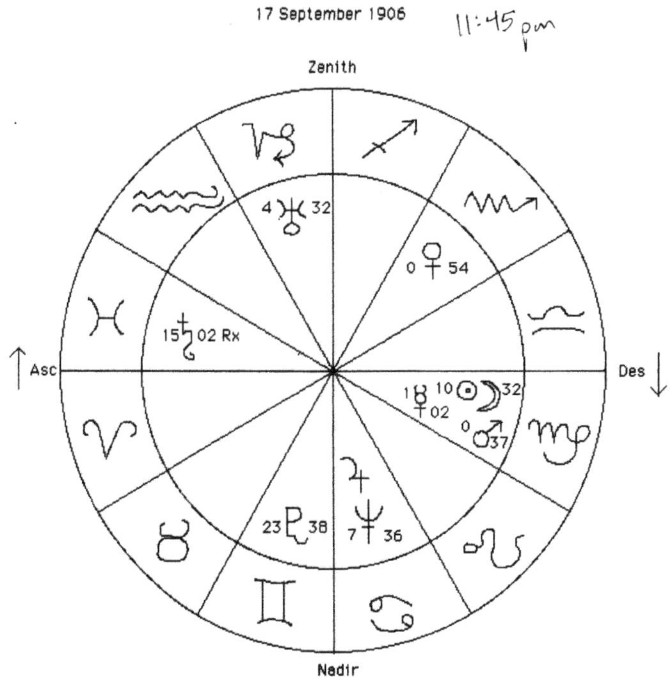

Santee Astrology

Santee showed signs of genius at an early age. By age 3 he would read both English and German. He learned Latin from his grandfather's grammar books. By age 8 he was translating Caesar's Gallic Wars from Latin into English and back again to check his grammar. He went to Wapwallopen High School and then on to Wilkes-Barre High School for his last year. He went to Central High School in Philadelphia for AB degree in Greek and had the highest score in the USA, and so went to Harvard.

At age 14 he was the youngest person to attend Harvard from 1924-26 where he graduated at age 16 with an AB Magna Cum Laude.

At Harvard he met EK Rand, the Latin scholar with whom he corresponded for years. When asked "Who interested you in the occult?", he cites Harvard teacher Professor Grandient who taught Medieval literature and old French, George L. Kitridge who taught English and TM Boura.

Harvard's Three Time Honor Winner

FREDERICK L. SANTEE

SANTEE LEADS SENIOR CLASS

Youngest Member of Harvard '24 Hails from Pennsylvania

Santee youth

He went to the University of Oxford England where he graduated age 18 in 1928 with an AB and then his MA in 1929. While at Oxford he jointed The Alpha et Omega Lodge of the Hermetic Order of the Golden Dawn where he met Aleister Crowley, HP Blavatsky, WB Yeats, Thomas Agee, Dion Fortune, AE Waite, and Israel Regarde. He also jointed Theosophical Society of England. At Oxford his main occult influence was from his philosophy teacher, a Professor Brabbart.

One source says he attended the University of Berlin in 1924-28 where he received his Ph.D. but this date does not seem to match the other records. He spent additional years in Rome, teaching positions at Harvard, Temple, Kenyon. Johns Hopkins, but held no tenure due to his socialist ideas. He was one of the 100 members of the Institute of Arts and Letters.

Santee as a young man

While at the University of Berlin he was initiated into witchcraft at a Coven 30 miles outside Berlin, the coven High Priest being an Arnold Reinman(d). In travels in the Middle East he met native adepts of the High Art in Egypt, learned from a German adept also in Egypt, and from a Sheik who was High Priest of a "coven" in

North Africa. Santee claims to have been a Homeopathic Doctor to Adolf Hitler but escaped Germany before the War. Santee also claims to have adopted into the USA the daughter of Hitler, named Tao, whom Hitler fathered to an English lady before the War.

In 1928 he married Edith Rundle from Allentown, Pa. In 1930 they either birthed or adopted a daughter names Ruth who died in 1938.

In 1930 he was a Sheldon Fellow and Fellow at the American Academy of Rome for 3 years. By then he could read Latin, Greek, German and some Sanskrit.

In the later 1930s he spent 6 years teaching in the USA at Lehigh, Vanderbilt, Harvard, Temple, and Kenyon colleges. As noted before he never achieved tenure at any of these institutions. During this time he jointed the America Roscicrucian Society and was initiated into the Illuminati degree.

In 1938 he graduated from John's Hopkins University in Baltimore Maryland with his MD degree.

From 1938-1942? he taught classical languages at Kenyon College in Ohio USA and was involved in the Humanistic Revival (see issues of the Kenyon Review). He opposed the US entrance into WWII since he was an avowed Socialist.

Also in 1942 he divorced Edith Rundle and married Betty Addis of Cumberland, Md. They adopted Tao. Betty died in 1966.

From 1943-45 he was drafted into the Navy, served in the South Pacific, but saw no action. Later stationed in Arkansas USA he was a Lieutenant in the Medical Corps. Also at that time he published "Sawdust and Tomatoes" (poems of his and his mothers).

The Harvard Yearbook of 1957 lists him as living in Baltimore practicing medicine there. From letters it appears he knew John Colhane the Irish writer, David McDowell at Kenyon and Random House, Father Flye from NYC, Clyde Pharr, and other famous classicists.

Santee aged 43

In 1956 Santee met Edna Jane Kishbaugh Williams aka Lady Phoebe Athene Nimue.

Santee and Phoebe - Soul Mates

In 1963 on his father's death, he returns to Wapwallopen Pennsylvania to continue his medical practice. His home and office were the same at 5 River Street.

Santee house/office

Santee Bookhouse

In the 1970s once the library was built next door he employed a total of 2 nurses and 4 secretaries and librarians. He wrote a newspaper column called: "The Country Doctor" and Janee wrote a column called:

"The Witches' Kettle". The locals says he was a kind and compassionate doctor, though a bit of an eccentric. He often treated the poor at no charge.

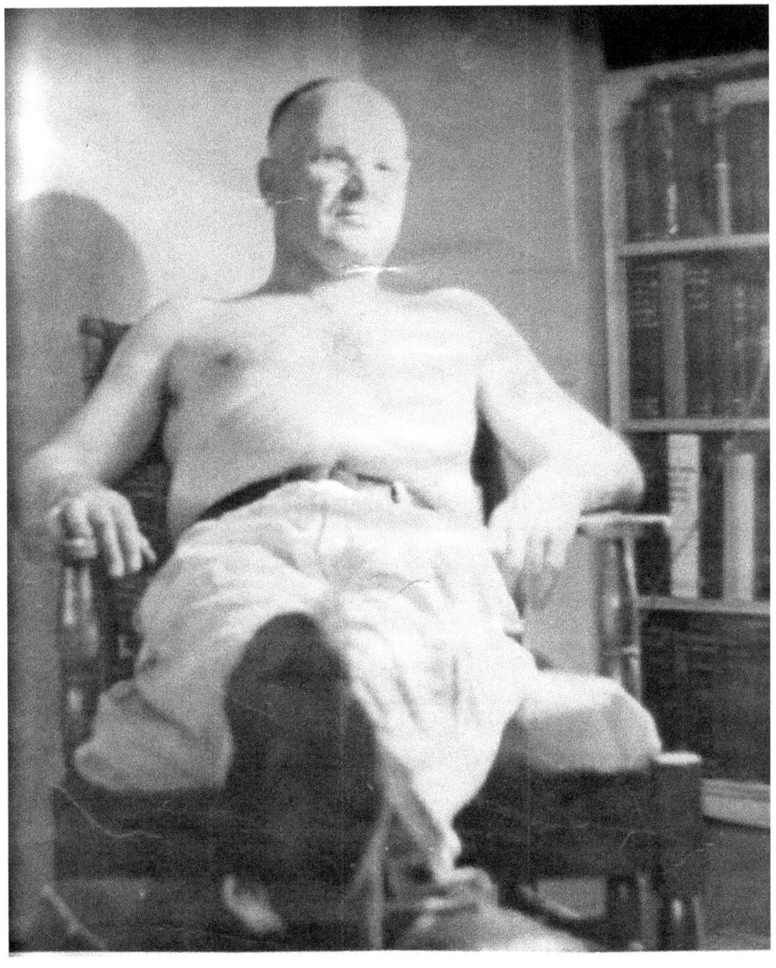

Herr Doktor

The Devil's Wager book cover
Exposition Press

Santee was known to have rubbed shoulders with much of the northeastern occult community. He was also a scholar of the Faust novels and legend and wrote his own Faustian story entitled "The Devil's Wager" set in modern times. He had a leg and nylon fetish if I can say so based on the amount of slides of ladies legs he had. He required his nurses and librarians to wear skirts, nylons and high heels at all times. He loves cats and all animals and supported the Humane Society and money from his will was donated to them. He was a regular to NYC and was known to frequent the Magickal Childe bookstore. He had met Sybil Leek at some time and invited her to his Covenstead. His ladies, foremost of which Phoebe, encouraged him to get initiated by her and start a Coven. In 1967 that happened and they received their charter from her. They titled the Coven of the Catta after the cat totem as I have written before and that coven continues to this day with a short hiatus of rituals from 1979, the year of the bookhouse fire through 1980 the year of his death. I wish I had arrived a few years earlier than I did to meet this intelligent, wonderful and weird man and magickian.

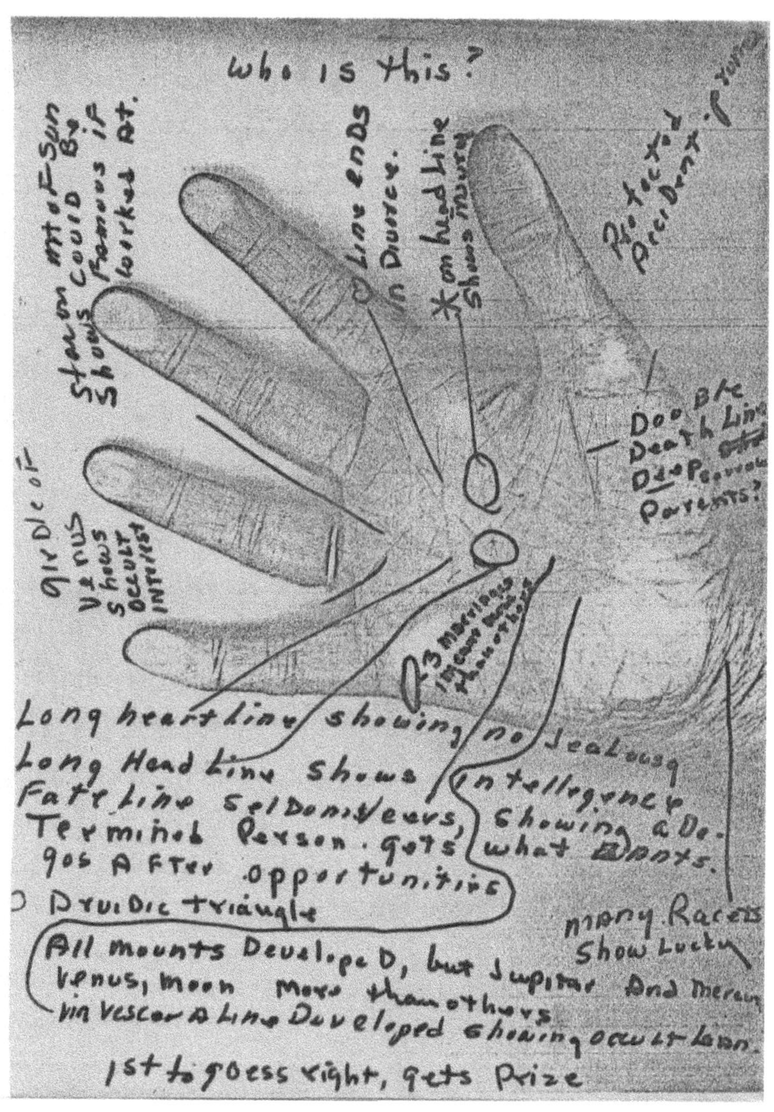

Santee Palmistry from

The Cat's Tale magazine

Dr Frederick LaMotte Santee died on 11 April 1980 aged 72 after a long battle with liver failure. His body is buried at the Old River Church just north of Wapwallopen, Pa. His gravestone says "I shall return when Spring's shadow trails."

Local scholar dies in Wapwallopen

Dr. Frederick L. Santee, 72, 5 River St., Wapwallopen, died at his home Friday at 10:35 p.m. following an extended illness.

A son of the late Dr. Charles L. and Verna Lloyd Santee, he began his practice in Wapwallopen in 1956. Prior to that, he had practiced medicine in Baltimore, where he also taught at Johns Hopkins University.

Dr. Santee was graduated from Harvard University, and Oxford University, England; Johns Hopkins Medical School, and universities in Berlin and Rome.

He was a classics scholar, who taught at Temple and Lehigh Universities.

Dr. Santee also wrote and published a number of books, the last being "The Devil's Wager."

A veteran of World War II, he served in the South Pacific.

His wife, the former Betty Addis, died in 1955.

He was the last surviving member of his immediate family.

Services will be held Tuesday at 1 p.m. from Old River Church, Wapwallopen, with the Rev. Chesley Laite, pastor of St. John's United Church of Christ, Wapwallopen, officiating. Burial will follow in the church cemetery.

The Heller Funeral Home, Nescopeck, is in charge of arrangements.

Santee Obituary

Old River Church and Graveyard

Photo by Michelle Beck

Santee Grave 2001 © GLH

Santee Biography Source Documents

From the Harvard Yearbook 25th Anniversary of the Class of 1924

Home address: 5078 Orville Ave., Baltimore 5, Md.

Office Address: 5200 Wright Ave., Baltimore 5, Md.

Born: Sept. 17, 1906, Wapwallopen, Pa.

Parents: Charles LaMotte Santee, Verna Caroline Lloyd

Prepared at: Central High School, Philadelphia, Pa.

Years in College: 1920-1924. Degrees: A.B. magna cum laude, 1924;

B.A. (University of Oxford), 1926; M.A. (ibid.) 1929;

M.D. (Johns Hopkins University), 1938

Married: Edith Rundle, Dec. 13, 1928, Allentown, Pa. (divorced 1942)

Betty Addis, 1942, Cumberland, Md.

Children: Ruth, March 18, 1930

(married W. J. McKnight, Feb 14, 1948).

Occupation: Physician.

Military or Naval Record: Lieutenant (Medical Corps) United States Naval Reserve, 1943-45.

His entry in the Harvard Year Book:

"I am the youngest member of the Class, probably the least successful, and possibly the only one who has never revisited Harvard. Perhaps these facts, on which my claim to uniqueness is based, are somehow interrelated. For years I kept up a correspondence, written largely in Latin, with my great teacher, the late Professor E. K. Rand. Writing Latin was the most valuable thing I got from Harvard. Many of you will, I fear, conclude that I got little else of value. My life has been beset with poverty and turmoil. It is a story of repeated attempts to root myself somewhere, of repeated failures to hold fast to my chosen career as a college teacher, in a world in which few can be taught, fewer still want to be, and a socialistic habit of thought reduces even those few to uniform patterns of empty gesture. Three lonely and studious years abroad -- the most strenuous of my life -- as a Sheldon Fellow and Fellow of the American Academy in Rome led to six years of precarious teaching at Lehigh and Vanderbilt. Surrounded constantly by a few devoted students, I did my real teaching extra-curricular, was ousted by the depression, and became first a Realsilk salesman, then a medical student. Immediately after graduation from medical school, I seized the first teaching position offered and for four years played a small part in the humanistic revival at Kenyon College. I opposed our entrance into World War II, was promptly drafted, and commissioned by the Navy in the Medical Corps. Three years of service here and in the South Pacific left me heavily in debt, since I had to support two families living in different places. By the end of the war, inflation and the needs of my dependents had advanced so far that I saw that the salary of an ordinary college professor would be inadequate. After four months of working with employment agencies, I could wait no longer. There was nothing to do but practice medicine. For low initial outlay and quick returns, I selected a government housing project on the outskirts of Baltimore. Before a year had passed, Stringfellow Barr and Scott Buchanon invited me to join them at St. John's on a salary I thought might suffice. The same year their finances collapsed and I had to buy back my old practice. Here I am in a dreary neighborhood, ministering to a demanding people, and more and more giving thought to their ills only for the sake of money I hope they will pay. I recognize that money is my only aim in life as it should have been from the start. In religion, I lean towards Anglo-Catholicism, am a member of no church. In politics, I believe in the decentralization of government and as little government as possible. I am a pre-New Deal Democrat."

From the Harvard Yearbook 50th Anniversary Class of 1924:

Frederick LaMotte Santee was born September 17, 1906, in Wapwallopen, Pennsylvania, the son of Charles LaMotte and Verna (Lloyd) Santee. He prepared at Central High School, Philadelphia, Pennsylvania, and received an A. B., magna cum laude, in 1924 at Harvard. He received a B. A. in 1926 at the University of Oxford and an M. D. in 1938 at Johns Hopkins University. His marriage in 1928 to Edith Rundle ended in divorce in 1941. In 1941, he married Betty Addis, who died in 1966. He had one child, Ruth, born in 1930 (deceased 1968), who married (1) William McKnight, (2) Juan Zaragoza, and (3) Alfred Jenanyen. There are two grandchildren. A physician, in general practice, Santee writes:

"If you don't know the poem that served as a model for these verses, you have not done a good job with your grandchildren:

How pleasant to know the good Doctor
Who writes all this horrible stuff; (1)
Some call him a scoundrel and rotter,
But a few think him pleasant enough.

His mind is abstract and fastidious,
His nose is remarkable big;
Were he only a little less hideous,
You would say he resembles a pig.

When he changes from far specs to near specs
The children are frightened and cry,
And their mothers shout, 'Hey! Don't you dare hex (2)
Poor Sam with your terrible eye!'

He has many friends, layman and clerical,
He sleeps every night with his cats,

His body is perfectly spherical,

His office girls never where flats. (3)

His office is unsanitary

With pictures of girls on the wall,

Every week he drinks gallons of sherry,

But never gets tipsy at all.

He is silent with people who talk a lot,

He won't look at women in slacks,

His favorite flavor is chocolate,

He rails at inflation and tax.

He hides in the depths of the cellar

While his patients call down through the flue,

'Come out of that cellar, you yeller,

You yeller old lazy bones, you!'

He reads, but he cannot speak, Spanish,
He still prefers women to men;
Ere the days of your pilgrimage vanish,
He hopes you will see him again.

Footnotes :

(1) Refers mainly to a newspaper column called the 'Country Doctor.'

(2) Actually he belongs to a coven of witches.

(3) A famous psychologist sees a relation between his fetish for high heels and his love of cats."

On rummaging through papers at the Library I also found a Master's Thesis that a visitor wrote about the Coven, containing the following bits of information I have copied verbatim:

Dr. Frederick LaMotte Santee:

Fourth generation Doctor

Grandfather in Civil War

Father graduated from LaFayette College and Jefferson Medical School in 1901, died 1963

Frederick attended Harvard at age 14 (youngest ever), graduated age 16, Oxford graduated 18, University of Berlin in 1924 for PhD, completed degree age 22, additional years in Rome, teaching positions at Harvard, Temple, Kenyon. Johns Hopkins, no tenure, one of the 100 members of the Institute of Arts and Letters

Knew German, Latin, Greek, English, Hebrew, could read Spanish, a little Sanskrit

Knew W.B.Yeats and Thomas Agee

In England initiated into the Golden Dawn and Theosophical Society

In USA Initiated into the Rosicrucian Lodge

Knew Crowley, Fortune, Regardie, Waite, and Blavatsky

Quote from the Thesis: "This interest in occult subjects seemed to culminate in his activities in the 'Coven of the Moon' in 'Little Town', where he could teach this knowledge. Although he did not care to practice ceremonial magic, he considered himself a teacher and researcher in many occult fields. He conducted experiments with a fair degree of success, but this was not his emphasis."

M.D. at Johns Hopkins in the 40's, on father's death returned to town to continue father's practice, dispensed his own medicines, office and home in same building, two nurses and four office girls, later investigated by the DEA.

Coven formed in 1963 under urging of head nurse "J".

On questioning individuals he seems to have been pushed into High Priest position to please his girls, charter for coven in 1967, although HPS should be leader actually Santee was the leader, instructed approximately 50 people during his Priesthood.

Believed he was a witch, but didn't believe in spirits because he never saw any, held a belief in a Universal Force he presumed to be God, felt that explanations of the psychic were in the individual instead of from outside forces, believed the Magick of Wicca is centered in male/female polarity, he was both social and solitary, he kept his thoughts and feelings to himself, kept his anger hidden, owned another house on mountaintop he'd retire to at times, his house/office in town being the center of activity in Wapwallopen, which was open to all as was the library also.

The Coven of the Catta Today

Over the decades there have been lots of stories told about the strange ole doctor and his coven. Some of these have taken on the style of what is called an urban legend. Some residents in the little town of Wapwallopen think he was a Satanist and his coven sacrificed cats. Reports of a supposed haunting in a house across the street from Santee's house and bookhouse brought in The Pennsylvania Paranormal Association and luckily I found out about this and gave my version of the story before it was filmed for the Animal Planet in a series called "The Haunted". The story is called "The Coven of the Cat" and you can view it on Youtube.com

The Coven of the Catta and I also have listings at Witchvox.com

Over the years various people have lived in Santee's house while the bookhouse continued to deteriorate and be vandalized. The property is now purchased by a new owner and being restored.

As I said the Coven of the Catta continues today with rituals still being held in Berwick and north of Harrisburg Pennsylvania. Here is a list of initiations after I arrived in 1981.

Image courtesy Adonis Merlin

Note – For the sake of privacy all living subjects, except for the author, are referred to only by their legal first name and/or their witch names.

From 1981-87 I (Gary Lee Hoke) was initiated into 1st degree as Shawnus, the 2nd degree as Merlin, and 3rd degree as Belarion. In 6/25/1988 Lady Phoebe Athene Nimue initiated me into the 3rd degree. She of course was initiated by Lord Merlin who was initiated by Lady Sybil. I initiated Lady Alsace Isa Brie into the 3rd degree. Alsace had been in the Coven for years beforehand. During my early years learning from Lady PAN I hand copies 3 Books of Shadows from the intact and fragmented BOSs that she had. After 9 years I turned the coven leadership over to others and continued to attend until the coven mostly fell apart. The Coven of the Catta continued with solitary witches in the Harrisburg area having occasional rituals using the format of those in the Books of Shadows and sometimes embellishing on those.

Here are the witches I have initiated. I initiated the females and the females initiated the males as per our tradition.

I initiated Iska Nuit Aradia (Patty) into her 1st and 2nd degrees. She was initiated into her 3rd degree by her husband Imago Alphanathea Satseteon (Bruce) who was initiated into all 3 degrees by his wife. They live in Harrisburg, Pennsylvania and no longer practice COC witchcraft that I know of.

I initiated Lady Alsace Isa Brie (Jeannie) into the 3rd degree 6/25/1998. She had previously been initiated into her 1st degree and 2nd degree by Lady Phoebe and Lord Merlin. She now lives in Berwick

Pennsylvania. She still practices the COC rituals with me.

Pheonix Lucan (Jeff) was initiated into his 1st degree by Lady PAN 6/1990, and later into his 2nd and 3rd degrees by Silver Ravenwolf of the Black Forest Coven lineage. He now lives near Carlisle, Pennsylvania. He is also a practitioner of German Powwow. He still occasionally practices the COC lineage rituals with me.

Chiram Abii (Steve) and Levanna (Kelly) were initiated in 1987 into their 1st degrees by me and Lady PAN and later were initiated as Naxul-Rael and Lavanara-Oshun into their 2nd degrees 6/28/1988. They later initiated each other into the 3rd degrees, then left the coven and now live in Maine.

I initiated Shambleau (Debra) 8/6/1989 into her 1st degree and then initiated her into her 2nd degree as Oya 3/10/1990. She still lives in York Pennsylvania.

I initiated Augur (Jeanette) into her 1st degree 2/2/1993, then she was initiated by Iska and her husband into her 2nd degree as Nagi 2/2/2003, and I initiated her into her 3nd degree as Astarte 4/3/2004.

Scores of people started their Probationerships but few of them went further. Lady PAN initiated Dave in the Berwick area into his first degree and possibly his second. I do not know his witch names. He died of an unfortunate accident falling down the cellar stairs and breaking his neck a few years ago.

In the winter of 2008-2009 I took all my hand written Books of Shadows and typed them into Word documents. All of the rituals were already in that format. This took months to do and they are now on CD and flash drives for COC initiates. Since then the BOSs have also been photographed page by page and are now in 3 PDF documents.

Three hand copied Books of Shadows

Now at age 57 I live with my two black cats in the mountains along a stream near Newport Pennsylvania. I still have my original Books of Shadows compiled from Lady PANs Books of Shadows, which I cherish. I occasionally do the COC rituals with Alsace, Phoenix and Adonis Merlin. Mostly I do the main rituals alone in my inside or outside temples. I have a good relationship with a handful of mostly 3rd degree witches in the local Black Forest Tradition.

I received permission from my elder Lady Alsace Isa Brie and the only other practicing 3rd* Lady Augur Nagi Astarte that it is time to share with the Black Forest Coven lineage of Silver Ravenwolf our rituals, formulas and spells, but not the initiation rituals or information only for a Probationer in the COC. This is based on what Lady Phoebe on her death bed told Lady Alsace when asked "what about the Coven?" her answer was "it's up to you". We can keep these seeds in a jar in the cellar, or sow them on the fertile ground of deserving, respectful, and initiated BFC High Priestesses and Priests.

In February of 2010 Lady Alsace and I have initiated Adonis Merlin (Matthew) into his 1st and 2nd degrees. He is presently taking on Probationers while I continue to only work with 3rd degrees in other lineages.

As far as I know the following people are still practicing he COC system - Alsace, Pheonix, Augur, Adonis and myself Shawnus. So as you can see the lineage of Dr. Frederick LaMotte Santee and Lady Phoebe Athene Nimue of the Coven of the

Catta continues strong to this day, growing, changing and initiating those who are worthy of this honor.

Blessed Be !

www.ingramcontent.com/pod-product-compliance
Ingram Content Group UK Ltd.
Pitfield, Milton Keynes, MK11 3LW, UK
UKHW020232250726
13967UKWH00001B/325

9 780557 859979